into the woods

Helen has travelled through 30 countries and has taught English as a second language in Ireland, England, Japan, China, New Zealand, and now online. She writes fiction, non-fiction, and poetry, and lives with her family in Lower Hutt, New Zealand.

Published by Piwaiwaka Press
First edition published 2022.
ISBN 978-0-473-62331-9
Second edition published 2023.
ISBN 978-0-473-67044-3
Copyright © Helen Mae Innes 2023

This book is copyright. Except for the purposes of fair review, no part may be stored or transmitted in any form or by any other means, electronic or mechanical, including recording or storage in any information retrieval system, without permission in writing from the publishers.

Artwork: Tama McArdell
http://tamamcardell.blogspot.com/

Cover design: Madden Hay

into the woods

helen mae innes

For a long time couldn't get out of bed, out the door, or out of my head. I looked at the bush through the window, my nose pressed to the glass, and listened to the muted voices of the birds. This, therefore, is my memoir from an alternate reality. Or, in other words, autofiction.

It happened during the spring when the kākā had first appeared in the valley. I noticed a grey warbler fledgling outside my window who couldn't get the tune quite right. He'd start singing, get a note wrong and falter, then try tentatively again. Like a child learning the recorder, I thought.

Like a child …

Each morning I waited in bed until the bird started singing. I held my breath wondering if that would be the day he finally got it right. Sometimes he'd almost make it all the way through until he'd hit a bung note and stop. It was his failure that endeared him to me. I didn't feel so bad for failing to get out of bed myself.

When he'd given up for the morning I'd sit on the edge of the bed and think, is this what it'll be like when I'm old? If I have dementia? Because I didn't know whether to stand up or lie down again. I had no purpose. Everything was heavy. Sometimes I just lay down again and closed my eyes. Delaying the start of the day.

Each morning when I got up I'd find Ivan had left some mail on the table in an apologetic little pile. He'd opened the ones addressed to both of us, the handwritten ones, so I didn't have to. There was never anything interesting but one morning a letter from the Royal Forest and Bird Protection Society lay on top. My parents had given me a membership as a Christmas present, but I kept forgetting this. The Society's personalised letters always surprised me but were welcome as if from an unsolicited, yet interesting sounding pen pal. They were having their annual Most Popular Bird survey, had I voted yet? I had not. I went out and sat on the back lawn and closed my eyes.

At that house I was surrounded by native bush and the trees were full of birds and their singing. The newly introduced kākā from the nearby bird sanctuary flew up and down the little valley where the streets wound up the hills like rātā vine. The first time I heard them screeching I felt like they were something prehistoric and dangerous, something like pterodactyls flying overhead. I'd tell myself I too celebrated their recent inclusion in the urban landscape, but instinctively I'd always hunch my shoulders and look furtively skyward.

I noticed there was something in my hand, fluttering in the breeze. I looked down. It was the flier. There were photos of all the contenders and labels declaring their conservation status: *In trouble. In serious trouble. Doing okay*. Am I in trouble? In serious trouble? *In trouble* means they might die out soon. Why don't they just say die?

Likely dead by the end of the week/year/decade. Might all die soon. Will most likely all die soon.

Die die die.

In the hospital they didn't say *die* either. They used euphemism after euphemism and Ivan didn't get it. He thought there was hope. He asked about treatment options, and the doctors looked uncomfortable, but still wouldn't cough up the unambiguous word. Ivan was not fluent in the language of death and I had to stop blubbing, suck in breath, and translate medical-speak into plain English.

Die, die, die. Death, death, death.

A grey warbler was singing in the distance. Probably not *my* grey warbler, as the tune was smooth and musical. There were lots of tūī there and kererū. I had grown up with dozens of kererū flying around the house, from kōwhai to kōwhai that my parents had planted outside each window. There were kererū and tūī outside the house and grey warblers in the bush behind. Harrier hawks overhead and moreporks called at night. My bird education wasn't explicit. I didn't know a lot about them except they were our neighbours, our friends, our whānau.

But that day on the lawn there were no kererū, the kākā had flown into the next valley, and the tūī were too busy swinging on the flax stalks sucking up nectar to be singing.

I looked down at the flier. The pictures were large, but the font was small and hard to read in the morning glare. I flicked through looking for the grey warbler but couldn't find it so had to start again, slowly turning the pages, carefully reading all the headings. When I finally found the grey warbler, I ticked the box then looked at the picture and thought, oh, is that what it looks like?

The grey warbler has always been my favourite bird, but until that moment, I had never actually seen one.

The grey warbler/riroriro is a tiny songbird and it calls out 'riro riro, riro riro' (gone gone, gone gone).

I read that and thought, of course he does.

I first saw what the riroriro looked like and understood what he was saying that spring – the spring I spent every day sitting alone on my back lawn grieving the loss of my tiny son who was gone gone, gone gone.

They had a small rental down the end of a cul-de-sac not far from their home. They said I could stay there until they found someone. But I knew they hadn't advertised, had kept it empty, just in case.

Mum had filled the flat with bookcases and filled the bookcases with books. Hundreds of them. Non-fiction on gardening, on native trees, birds, fungi, wars, history, sunken treasure, conspiracy theories, dog training, mediation, time management. Old journals full of academic articles on precise and obscure topics. Novels, short stories, poetry, plays, in English, and in languages I knew no one in the family spoke.

My mum passed me books the way others pressed comfort food into my hands.

I liked being there. Which was surprising. I had travelled the world to avoid living in that type of house, in that type of street, amongst that type of people. But once the novelty of accents had worn off I realised that type of person was everywhere, and I was one of them.

There was a whole section of books with respelt dialects I recognised as having come from my parents' house. Books I'd found impossible to read when at home I began to read with dread, then delight. I read *Trainspotting* by Irvine Welsh and *How Late It Was, How Late* by James Kelman and remembered knocking on Edinburgh doors with my CV and being told I wouldn't want to be there in the winter, that no one wanted to be there in the winter, and not getting a job there. I finally read *A Clockwork Orange* and realised Anthony Burgess's linguistic talent for finding words in Russian to use as new slang in English was brilliant. The impenetrable writing was suddenly not only meaningful but funny. Dating a Russian had been good for this and then I read Dostoevsky and finally understood the patronymic naming system.

But all the novels were depressing, and I decided to leave literature behind for a while.

My mother's home cataloguing systems were odd. At first seemingly chaotic but themes emerged in the same way meaning slowly seeps from a poem with rereading. Novels were not shelved all together. The novels with respelt dialects were with books about birds, and works on and by Shakespeare, on public speaking, watch repair, nautical flags, an LP of NZ birdsong,

Dylan Thomas, coding, code breaking, Yeats, communication between animals.

So, I read about gibbons.

Elephants and whales and gibbons. They all communicate. Gibbons tell each other if a tiger is coming, or if a bird is coming. They whisper the *bird warnings* at a frequency the birds can't hear. They talk about finding food. The males talk to new neighbours, while the females ignore them. They remind me of an old married couple.

She looks and sounds like a gibbon: too much mascara; long naked limbs no thicker at the armpit than at the wrist. She speaks too low for him to hear. He squints and adjusts his hearing aid, knowing she is whispering words with consequences, screaming phrases of no significance.

He is too deaf.

She is too quiet.

She says something, under her breath, and takes his silence as acceptance. Sandwiches appear instead of casserole for tea. His comfy corduroy chair disappears to be replaced by something with levers and giant velvet flowers. He knows if he complains she'll insist she'd told him and that he never listens.

Mum rang to say she'd organised for the Remutaka Forest Park Ranger to speak to the local Historical Society about pest control in the area, and the time I should be there. There's a lovely supper afterwards, she said. It'll be interesting.

It wouldn't, I thought. I didn't go. I let my mother down, but I really couldn't face standing in a cold community hall with a bunch of olds listening to how to catch possums, stoats, and rats. I've never seen my parents more excited than when they gave each other rat catching devices for Christmas and insisted on setting them up after our lunch. One attached to a tree and drove a bolt into the brain of the rat who ventured under it, and the other was a high-tech cage which informed you by text when to empty it. The only reason my dad kept his cell phone charged was for those texts.

I'd never shared their love for pest eradication. Well, that's what I told myself but really, I just didn't want to be around people. Any people.

But I dutifully phoned later that evening, out of politeness, and asked how it went. She said that the ranger whistled the bird calls (he was very good) and he talked about the difference in bird dialects in Wainuiomata versus the Hutt Valley. And I don't know why but that the idea of birds having dialects stuck.

There were so many books in the house but sometimes it was as though they were all in other languages. I have always loved books. Slept with books, the weight of them on the blankets comforting me. Waking up with them on my pillows was such joy. The smell of them as I flicked through the pages like a faint puff of woody perfume every few minutes. But I got to the stage where I couldn't find anything I wanted to read. I didn't want to read about people and their lives. They were either too happy, or too depressing. Gibbons are a little too much like people talking. Whales reminded me of babies swimming in embryonic fluid. But I did feel I could read about birds even though it was something I knew nothing about. Or maybe because of it.

But I hated birds. At a basic, visceral level. I loved them for their symbolic representation of nature and recognised the importance of their conservation. I hated them as feathered, shitty, stupid, diseased flying rodent/dinosaur hybrid monster things. I wished I lived in, well anywhere really, somewhere where I could choose moose or wolves or squirrels or badgers or snakes or monkeys or crocodiles or anything else to be interested in, to be in love with, to be fascinated by. But New Zealand only has birds. And I hated birds so much.

It's not a popular view. Somehow not patriotic. Somehow a sign of not caring about nature. I loved nature, just not birds, but I knew enough to keep it to myself.

Why did I hate them? I'd never questioned it before, even though I lived in a country that worshipped them. Maybe I just I hated bird poo? There was that incident with the bird poo when I was eating a fillet-a-fish in Midland Park back when there was that waterfall and there were pigeons and pigeon poo everywhere. The pigeons are still there even if the waterfall has gone. I was a teenager and so horribly anxious about everything I thought everyone was staring and judging me even though there was no reason for anyone to even notice me. I had wanted to go to a café but in a café, you need to talk to someone and know what to order and they were dark mysterious places with strange names for coffee. So I went to McDonalds, even though I hated McDonalds. I had a fillet-a-fish in my hands and somehow

I got tartar sauce on my hand. How did that happen? So I licked it off and immediately realised it was poo! But I couldn't spit it out or wipe my mouth with a serviette because then everyone would know I'd just licked pigeon poo off my hand! So I ate it. And hated myself for doing so.

It's hard being the centre of the universe. Teenagers have a tough time of it. But when I remember it, I am that teenager again. I feel that shame again and my hatred for pigeons.

Did I hate birds before then?

Remember the geese? There was a gang of geese in the middle paddock until I was about four. No, not a gaggle, that word sounds sweet, like a cuddly group of grandmas gossiping. A group of geese is a gang. Geese meant not ever going anywhere near that paddock and walking the long way around to get to the shearing shed. Geese meant fear. Geese still mean fear.

And then there was that trip to Kapiti Island as a kid when a weka had run off with the precious bag of scroggin. The only source of chocolate I had as a kid was being stolen, secreted away into the bush. It was the only time I have ever seen my mother run and the first time I ever heard her swear.

Yay for conservation, and animals and nature. But geese can go and fuck themselves and become extinct. I hate geese. I really, really, hate geese. I was glad when I heard that New Zealand had had a native goose but it had gone extinct. I cheered.

And then I felt bad.

And then there was the cockatoo in a cage somewhere when we were on holiday in Matamata. I went with my friend's family, so I was on my best behaviour. My friend was patting one bird and bored of watching, waiting, I stuck my finger through the cage bars to pat the other one, though didn't really want to. The thing is, when a cockatoo bites a finger it's not like a puppy mouthing your hand playfully. It's a screaming, swearing experience. It's a fucken hell kind of thing as the blood starts to run and yet the bird is still hanging on. It's not long really by the counting of the second hand on a watch, but it is a bloody long time when measured by the number of pain messages that are sent along the peripheral nervous system to the spinal cord and up to the brain. It's a no buses come and then they all come at once kind of thing. With pain usually being not only all the buses come at once but not one of them is using their brakes, so they all slam into each other and there's body parts and twisted metal and pools of blood everywhere. And then the cockatoo lets go and there's a moment of stillness, a silence, staring at the blood gushing out and then there's the thump thump thump inside the finger as all the blood pushes and shoves to get out, like revellers escaping a nightclub bombing through partially blocked fire doors.

I might be exaggerating.

But I hate birds and I hate bird poo, and I really hate geese. Little fuckers.

But there were sounds outside my window: teenagers on their way to parties, neighbours chatting over the fences, mothers calling their kids in for tea, and birds. Birds calling in alarm at cats playing statues in the undergrowth, singing to would-be lovers, mimicking the sounds of the cell phones, the washing machines, the man next door who whistles while he washes down his gumboots. I thought he was always washing his gumboots until I noticed the tūī in the kōwhai singing the same tune. I slunk down below the level of the windowsill.

But the birds sang outside my window and it felt like the least intrusive of the sounds and the only one somehow directed at me.

The same section in the bookshelf that had all the dialects had *Peter Rabbit* and *The Wind in the Willows*, both of which I hated as a kid. That's not my kind of thing at all. Though, I did love the darker *Watership Down* ... I kept thinking, as I read about all these animals in waistcoats with their relationships and dramas, what do birds talk about? What does the voice of a bird sound like?

Sometimes when I was younger, walking home from school, if I bumped my left hand against a fence railing I would have to bump my right hand too, to even things up. Or if I stood on a tree root with one foot, or scratched my head, or bit my tongue, or did anything on one side somehow I'd find a way to redress the imbalance. Sometimes it was quite awkward. I didn't think about it much, but knew, or suspected enough to know, to hide it from others, hide it from myself even.

I had forgotten about that compulsion to steady myself. That feeling of being slightly queasy, uneasy. But that's the feeling I had that spring.

The first book I read was exactly in the centre of the centre shelf, at eye level. And I had to read all the books on the shelf directly in the middle and from the middle outwards. To be even. I tried not to think about it too much. I tried not to let it worry me. But I read a lot of books I wouldn't have read otherwise.

My parents like birds, own a lots of books about birds. So, I ended up reading a lot of books about birds.

I read about bird dialects as though it was the most interesting thing on the planet.

No, that's not quite right either, but I read about birds as though it is the only thing I could tolerate. Not stuff with people in it. I even read about maths, about swarm algorithms for starling murmurations, and about the physics of sound.

I have no background in physics, failed statistics repeatedly, much to the disbelief and disgust of my Russian husband, and only did biology till sixth form. I knew nothing about birds or how they produced sound or how sound is perceived by humans, and only have basic musical ability, but in between the jargon and the statistics and the new concepts

I started picking things up, while successfully avoiding:
interacting with people,
reading about people,
thinking about people.

I read *What the Robin Knows* by Jon Young, a bird language expert in the United States who trained in the Native American tradition of tracking. He runs workshops and travels the world learning bird languages from indigenous peoples. In his book he explains that if you want to see wolves, bears, mink, moose, etc. then you need to watch what the birds are doing. Unless you are careful the birds will tattle on you, telling all these other species that you are in the forest, and then you'll see nothing of interest.

It's not just their calls, but their movements that will let everyone know what is happening. There's the obvious stuff like if they fly from a lower to a higher perch a ground predator is passing and if they fly from the treetops down to a hidden branch then a flying predator is around. But Young uses birds to see what other creatures are in the forest. Exciting creatures like wolves, bears, foxes, beavers. Creatures I was brought up with, in fairy tales, in cartoons, in books. Although, outside of a zoo, they were creatures I could never expect to see. In New Zealand all we have is birds.

I was jealous of Young's knowledge, desired it, even though it is not so useful here. But I still had no desire to buy binoculars or guidebooks or sit in hides.

So I was encouraged when, despite being seemingly more knowledgeable about bird behaviour than many others I'd read, he said we don't need special equipment, just a notebook and a willingness to be observant. I just wanted to be more observant, and he said to do that you should get a *sit spot* less than two minutes from your house and go there every day. Just sit and watch.

I can do that, I thought. I'm already sitting. I'm not going anywhere.

So I started watching the birds. Sitting on the couch looking out the window. Sitting on the top step looking at the garden.

As well as the floor to ceiling shelves full of books there were handwoven baskets from Trade Aid bulging with magazines: *Scientific American, Forest and Bird, National Geographic, New Zealand Geographic, Wilderness, Kiwi Gardener*. Whichever magazine I picked up there was some article about nature being healing, about *forest bathing,* or the effects of the sounds of birdsong on the brainwaves. Instead of taking antidepressants people should go for a walk in the forest.

I didn't know if my mother had chosen all those magazines deliberately or whether those types of articles were just popping up everywhere. I especially remember one study where a group of researchers from the Netherlands looked at the effects of the forest on participants who didn't even go into the forest. They were merely shown photos of either urban built spaces showing streets, houses, cars, or green urban spaces such as parks, gardens, leisure areas, and grassy fields before or after a stress test (a maths test! Of course it was!) and measured their bodies' abilities to recover from the stressful events. Green photos helped them more.

The thing is though, when I looked at the photos in the article I thought that the green spaces were so boring, unnatural, unwild looking that they made me depressed. They reminded me of travelling, feeling desperate for lush bush, for wild untouched spaces. I would seek out parks shown as green geometric shapes on maps, and find trees in rows surrounded by browning grass with women pushing old-fashioned looking prams and I would feel lost and alone and very, very far from home.

But I was glad to read that mere photos could help. I didn't feel so bad about never leaving the house, about lying on the couch looking up at the bush-clad hills.

I knew that it would be good to go for a walk in the bush. I love the bush. I always feel better there. Even just thinking about bushwalks others had dragged me along on in my lifetime I feel better. But I never went myself. I could have walked up the road for only two minutes and been at the start of the Rātā Loop Walk. But I didn't. There were countless articles telling me the climate is changing, a huge number of native birds are on the edge of extinction and their numbers are getting worse, the rivers are so polluted the algae is killing dogs and we can't go swimming anymore. I wanted to save the environment, I knew it was important, but it's depressing. Looking at forests reminds me of deforestation. Better to watch a sci-fi movie about distant planets.

I didn't want to think about the birds, the fish, the mammals, and the planet dying. So, I turned the statistics I read into a happy tune, a joyful carol, and hummed it repetitively:

Since Human Settlement

Since human settlement
New Zealand has lost
fifty one birds
four plant species
three frogs
and three lizards
one fresh water fish
reptiles, frogs, and snails
the short-tailed bat
and far more are now endangered.

Go for a walk, they said, it will do you good. Actually, nobody said that to me. People knocked and ran. I opened the door to find comfort food in dishes on the doormat: eggplant parmigiana, shepherd's pie, sticky date pudding, spaghetti and meatballs, potato gratin, seafood risotto, chicken and leek pie, zucchini quiche, macaroni and cheese. Like famous killers the dishes all had more than one name. I never knew who had delivered any of it. An acquaintance with an excellent memory had tracked down friends and colleagues and scheduled them all for deliveries of food. One friend who did venture inside sat uneasily in my kitchen and admitted he wouldn't have visited if he hadn't been bullied into it. He drank the tea while it was still scolding and left.

Later I sat on the grass. It was the furthest I'd ventured from the house for ages. The birds sang. I didn't think about anything. Ivan didn't talk to me. I didn't talk to him. There was nothing to say. The birds sang. And I found I wanted to know what they were saying. My shelves were full of bird books. There are always magazines and books around. But when I opened the guidebooks there was a coldness.

I closed all the windows. I couldn't hear the birds anymore. I gazed down the valley at the fog rolling in from the south. Maybe I fell asleep. Maybe Ivan came home from work and threw a blanket over me. Maybe the birds all went to sleep too.

Advice for friends of the recently bereaved

What to do… Firstly, you need to train. Long runs, rides or swims will give you stamina, but what you really need is speed. Practise sprints from one lamppost to the next. Pump your arms. Push down and away with your feet. Run like your life depended on it. Remember, death is catching. Or something. It's a bit vague, actually. Just make sure you take food in a bag with a tea towel at the bottom or better yet put the food in tupperware so you can drop it quickly without fear of anything breaking. Practise your sprints down the plastics aisle at Briscoes.

Drop the food and run.
Run.
Run like the wind.

In the beginning is denial. Deny everything. Deny friendship, deny food, deny sleep – no, actually, don't deny sleep, sleep far too much. Sleep sleep sleep. Sleeping is the ultimate in denying reality. Learn how to absolutely turn off and lie in bed for hours longer than necessary.

There is silence and not silence. Working my way along the shelf I picked up a book called *The Art of Mindful Silence* by Adam Ford. Finally, a book I wanted to read!

But it wasn't about silence at all. His advice was all about going into the forest, going to the beach and I thought, don't you know how bloody noisy those things are? Nature is noisy as fuck. The beach with all the stones knocking against each other, the waves pummelling down, that's noisy man.

And it never stops. It never stops. It's exhausting just thinking about it. It's not like a forest with ebbs and flows of birdsong and if you cut down a forest the sounds are gone. You can make it stop at least. But the sea? The beach? It's forever and somehow that makes the noise worse.

What the author meant was getting away from people talking. That's a good start I suppose but it's not silence.

I read *The Great Animal Orchestra* by Bernie Krause until I got to the bit about the beaver. Krause recorded soundscapes all over the world. With soundscapes you can tell the health of an environment by seeing if all the sound frequencies are full of the noises of life. Unhappy ecosystems have gaps where the sounds of some creature who evolved to sing in it has gone.

Then he tells the story of the worst sound he ever recorded. A ranger decided to use TNT to destroy a beaver dam and the sound the male beaver made when he returned to find his mate and babies blown to bits was the most heart-wrenching of his career. I closed the book and yearned for silence, even if silence is a sign of something missing.

The clock on the wall was bloody noisy. It had belonged to a great aunt in Christchurch and before her an ancestor from the old country had carried it in on a ship. The clock taunted me, reminding me that life was ticking away, one second at a time. Ticking away till my own inevitable death. Ticking away until I had to return to my job. Ticking away all those seconds taking me further and further away from my baby. The clock in the hospital had been especially egregious, ticking away those seconds when I still held him but moving towards the point when I had no choice but to bury him. The clock stealing away my time with him.

They told me to take photos of him. For the memories, they said. I kept saying I didn't want photos of a dead baby. They wouldn't listen. It wasn't on their checklist of approved or acknowledged cultural beliefs. My husband frowned. You don't take photos of dead people. The midwife smiled, laughed, and said, He has a funny accent, doesn't he? I can't understand a word he's saying!

She took photos of my baby anyway and gave them to me on a memory stick. Research has proved it's beneficial, she said. *Stick that*, I thought. But I didn't say that. I kept quiet.

In *Every Word is a Bird we Teach to Sing*, Daniel Tammet interviews a Nahuatl speaker who tells him the clock says, *Work this, work that*. It certainly has an impatient tone so I can believe it. The clock demanded I go back to work the same way my boss kept ringing and telling me to get back to work immediately if I want to keep my job, telling me, Maternity leave is for mothers with babies. So I didn't want to listen to the clock ticking anymore.

I opened the windows and a cicada sang the same tune I remembered from childhood,

W-h-a-t a-r-e you gonna do-o-o-o?
W-h-a-t a-r-e you gonna do-o-o-o?

I'd picked up a book about physics, about sound waves. I never studied physics, but I did do chemistry for a few weeks. The problem was I just couldn't believe that atoms existed. I told Mr Reid he needed to convince me that atoms existed before I would, or could, learn the periodic table.

Mr Reid was nice. He couldn't understand how I wouldn't accept that atoms existed, and I couldn't understand how he could just take something on faith.

Prove it, I said. This is a science class, isn't it? It's not religion, so don't ask me to just believe.

Well, he said, if we looked through an electron microscope, we could see them.

I'd wanted to know if we had an electron microscope in the classroom. He'd laughed.

No, the school budget doesn't stretch to that.

Have you ever looked through an electronic microscope? I asked.

Ahh, no. No, I haven't.

He looked wistful.

Finally, one day about a month into the course, he excitedly asked if I knew about Rutherford's radiation experiment conducted with a sheet of finely beaten gold. He explained it quickly and simply. Alpha particles were fired at gold foil and most went through and were detected behind the foil, but some bounced off something and that something was conjectured to be the nucleus of the atom. Most went through since the atom is mostly empty space.

Oh. Okay. That makes sense. Yup, I believe in atoms now.

He was astonished, and happy! The methodology of the experiment made sense to me as proof that atoms existed, the story had convinced me just as well as an electron microscope might have been expected to.

Good, can you please learn the periodic table now?

No, sorry.

He didn't want me to quit his class but I

pointed out if it took a month for me to accept that atoms existed then I might not have enough time for him to think up examples to convince me of every little thing I needed to learn. I didn't know if I could learn to take information on faith.

But that spring I kept thinking about the crossover between physics and spirituality. How everything is connected. How little bits of you are flying off and becoming part of me and how little bits of me are flying off and becoming part of you. How if atoms are mostly empty space then so are we. About how you should invite a physicist to speak at a funeral because he or she could explain that energy doesn't die, that energy is neither created nor destroyed. I kept reading about multiverses and thinking about how in another universe my baby didn't die.

I didn't know where the energy that was my baby had gone. And I didn't know how to get a physicist to speak at his funeral.

And maybe little bits of the birds and the

bush were flying off and becoming part of me and little bits of the people walking past my door were flying off and becoming part of the birds.

Where does the table end and where do I begin? If atoms are mostly empty space why can't I push my finger through the table? I was reading about boundaries and thinking about where one suburb starts and another ends, about where one language begins and where it ends. When does it become a new language and when is it just a dialect? Where is it still mutually understandable and where do you throw up your hands and say, I don't understand!

In Japan they would look at my face and say, *Wakarimasen! Eigo o hanashimasen*, even though I was speaking Japanese, not English, so why didn't they understand? I'd see it happening with others too who were fluent, even with my American-Japanese friends. So, how much of comprehension is attitude and preconception, and how much of it is sound?

Where does the bush end and where do I begin?

Maybe the birds are talking but we think they're just saying, Tweet tweet tweet.

Maybe we're ignoring the fact they're saying stuff?

We think the gibbons are just screaming but they're saying, A tiger is coming! Or, The coast is clear!

Acacia trees emit ethylene to tell each other when antelopes are around so they can up their poisonous content as a result. The smell of freshly cut grass is actually the grass screaming out to other grass, Watch out! The sheep/lawnmower/grass murderer is coming!

Maybe we are throwing up our hands in front of feathered friends and saying, I don't understand! I don't speak bird!

And maybe they're looking at us with contempt.

When everyone was at work and the flow of cars down the hill had dried up, I sat on my lawn in the sun. I sat there to get away from the clock, seeking silence, but the birds were in the bush.

It was spring and they were singing again. The riroriro was singing, announcing it was time to plant. Time to get life started again, the winter weather will be gone soon. The spring flowers were coming up and the first lambs over the fence were bouncing in the paddocks. Announcing, despite the icy rain, that summer was on its way.

I should buck up too, I thought. The birds were calling but I couldn't see them. The bush was green and brown, and the birds were green and brown, and I couldn't tell them from the leaves. I wondered if the bush was too dense or I was too dense. I didn't know how people bird watch.

A book I found on my shelves called *Last Child in the Woods* by Richard Louv says to feel happier we should go into the woods, the forest, to see the birds. Forest birds are in the forest not on the edge, this edge where the woods and suburbia meet.

Except we call it the bush, not woods. And the birds in his book are red, are blue, are bright yellow. Seemingly impossible colours for birds.

The house was at an intersection of native bush, cleared pastoral land and encroaching suburbia. I was at a crossroads. Was I forging a path into nature, encroaching, trespassing, or holding suburbia back? The stopper in the dyke perhaps? A place where people, domestic animals, and wildlife met. Except no one met me there. No one was talking to me except the birds and I couldn't see them.

I figured I could wait there for another food delivery left by a fleeing friend or I could flee into the woods.

The bush has always been a nice backdrop to my life. It makes for wonderful views. It raises the price of real estate. Leafy suburbs are desirable suburbs. All that greenery made me believe I was in a healthy neighbourhood. The trees produce oxygen, cleanse the city air, comfort the soul.

But I rarely went into bush and I never *went bush*.

I used to walk a wide track through the botanical gardens taking me from one vibrant suburb to another, or along the town belt, or through a park. Kelburn down to the CBD, Brooklyn to Aro Valley, Newtown to Kilbirnie. But these are managed green spaces with birdsong as ambient background noise rather than true bush. It's definitely not wilderness. I realised on my travels that I thought I wanted wilderness but really, I wanted a certain shade of green, the correct crinkling of the hills, the reassurance of nature as backdrop.

The normal world was out there. The clocks and the jobs and the traffic and the mortgages and the death. Especially the death. Death in suburbia means funerals with piped fake Celtic music despite the fact I had said no music, and graveyards with permanent marble reminders, and sympathy cards arriving along with the mortgage demands. The death regrets and the death pledge mixing together.

Death is a permanent feature in suburbia. In the forest it's there and then it's gone. The body falls to the ground, it gets covered in leaves, the gut bacteria grows, the abdomen extends, the body rots, the skin slides off, the flies come, the beetles come, the scavenging birds and animals come, then the wind and rain erosion takes the last of the flesh then the bones away and there is nothing left but fertilised ground ready for the next life.

There is death and then there is life again.

The bush is a dreamlike place with filtered light turned green by the leaves. The bush has filtered sound muted by the humid air and dense foliage. The sounds in the northern forests, in Europe, in Russia, in North America, travel further and clearer. The sounds made by New Zealand birds have to be higher, louder just to be heard.

The bush was not the basement with its boxes of unused clothes, of baby things I couldn't bear to part with. The bush was not the bedroom with its blankets that muffle the sounds of visiting family.

She's sleeping, they'd say. Do you think she's sleeping too much?

In the bush the birds are no longer the backdrop but the thing. The bush is not the trees. The bush is not the birds. The bush is not fungi nor ferns nor invertebrates. The bush is all these things. Take one group out and it's no longer the bush.

If you ever need someone to talk to …

Except that involves call and response, turn-taking, conversation. I didn't need someone to talk to. I needed someone to talk to me with no compulsion on my part to reply, to take my turn, to show any sign of having listened to a word they'd said.

The birds were talking to me and didn't give a flying fuck if I was listening or not. In the bush birds are blatant in their disregard for my sensibilities.

Fuck! Watch out! Some clumsy human is walking this way!

There was no subtlety in the way they told each other things. They didn't try to spare my feelings. They're the worst of the bare faced bullies …

Or … if I'm not seeking to take offence … they just tell it how it is.

Just as a snowplough brutally shoves aside any snow, I *did* set off what Krause called a *bird plough*. My oblivious stomp through the undergrowth to a sit-spot resulted in a Mexican wave of rising and falling birds accompanied by yelling and complaining calls. And then it all settled down again.

Every day I walked to the same sit spot. Barely into the bush but far enough that I was hidden from my house and the people who dropped and ran. Jon Young had said to find a sit spot, so I forced myself out the door and into the bush each day. There I could watch people come, set down the casserole dishes quietly, arrange the card carefully on top, steady themselves, knock and run away. Some of them fairly sprinted. It was impressive. I didn't mind anymore. They ran from their sides of the same conversations I was hiding from. I closed my eyes.

Young says to not rush, but I couldn't help myself in the wild scrabble up the little hill each day. Don't rush and yet don't tiptoe, don't creep. Don't move as a cat would move, sliding along, stealthily. That is the way of a predator. Move with calm movements.

I can't promise that, I whispered to the book. It was all I could do to drag myself out of the house. It was a wonder I was there at all in that green world.

I did the same each day. Not so much running towards the bush as away from the bungalow. I kept reading about people who loved birds. Birdwatchers who will spend hours watching them, taking notes, sketching images, travelling vast distances to see rare species. There were lovers of pet birds, birdbaths, birdfeeders, bird calls on the radio to announce the start of the news.

I knew people loved birds but I couldn't quite understand it yet. Couldn't feel it. I thought of birds in more of a bad omen way. In a bird flu, bird brained, Hitchcock way. In a bitter way.

I realised, anger scares the birds away. I scare the birds away. I am anger.

People kept asking me whose fault it was. Did a midwife make a mistake? Did the obstetrician? Did the hospital?

No, no, no.

And then they looked at me in a way I didn't like and wanted to know what I had eaten, had I exercised too much or too little, had I drunk, smoked, or fucked too much?

No. Sometimes babies just die.

I said this a couple of times, and they looked at me like they didn't believe me. Like I was lying, covering something up. Everyone wanted someone to blame while I just wanted to grieve. So, I found a spot higher up on the hill, harder to get to, in need of much more clambering, struggling, of my being scratched and made dirty. I found somewhere to sit where I didn't have to watch people come and go to my house, or worse, increasingly, people not come and go.

One day I couldn't go into the bush. I had to see my obstetrician and afterwards I could wait in the rain or in a café for Ivan to pick me up. I would rather have sat in the rain, but Ivan would have lectured me for a week about getting cold, getting sick. The café was full of straight lines and 90-degree angles and bright colours and weird noises that I realised were people talking. I had not been in a café for a long time.

A barista moved with non-threatening movement. I didn't know why he was so gentle setting down my coffee, as though the cup, the saucer, the table and me on my chair would all shatter into splinters at the merest breath of wind. It was certainly not the movement of a predator. I puzzled over the barista until I remembered that when I had entered the café I'd met a seldom seen colleague from another department in the queue. She looked at my belly then congratulated me,

You've had your baby! Having a quick break are you? It's so tiring, isn't it? What did you have?

The barista had heard my reply.

There's no baby. He died.

I was so tired. I was too tired to be angry anymore.

When I was angry the birds were angry back. It was alarm calls all the way down the valley and I longed for bird song. I decided not to be angry with the world anymore. Not to be angry with all the people who said,

Oh how terrible!

How horrible!

Oh, that sucks!'

I wanted softly spoken words, delicately worded phrases. So, I stepped gently through the undergrowth. The barista had moved not with stealth but with love and concern. He hadn't asked me whose fault it was or why or how. Jon Young said you should walk through the forest with respect, feeling neither threatening nor needy.

The barista would make a good bird watcher, I thought.

So, I learned to walk in the bush in a way that didn't scare the birds by mimicking a barista softly placing a teacup for a bereft mother who was somehow also not a mother. I entered the forest, moving like a stranger not wanting to spill a drop, with a calm respectful grace.

I read a book about angry birds. Angry birds are always funny, even if they are not spherical cartoons. The Mincing Mockingbird wrote *Guide to Troubled Birds*, with pictures of birds giving sarcastic advice, telling tragic anecdotes, being evil, swearing. It made me laugh. The first time in ages. There's something funny about pissed off birds telling it how it is.

The Nahuatl speaker in *Every Word is a Bird we Teach to Sing* says that birds have dirty mouths. But he doesn't say what. And another author suggests birds say unspeakable things but also doesn't elaborate.

I wanted to know what foul-mouthed birds say. I was sick of euphemisms and tiptoeing around topics.

The doctors kept beating around the bush so Ivan had hope, was asking about treatment.

When would it start? Why hadn't they started already?

And they still wouldn't bloody tell him. It was euphemism after euphemism. So, I had to tell him. I had to stop crying and translate:

We're sorry, into, He will die.

Translate pregnant pauses and pitiful looks, into, He will die.

Wipe snot off my face and translate, It's not looking good, into, He will die.

So, if the birds have dirty mouths, I wanted to damn well know what it is they were saying. The authors of various books might think it's bad form, but believe me, I've heard worse.

My boss visited despite all my colleagues running interference for weeks trying to stop him. A phone call gave us five minutes warning, so Ivan and I hid behind the sleep-out. The morepork in the bush behind us woke and called. The moreporks in the north of our suburb called, Morepork! While those in the south called, Ruru!

But the one behind our house always said, in an exasperated tone, Arsehole!

It made us giggle.

The next time I was on the hill watching the bush, watching the lambs grow bigger I listened out for angry birds. I wasn't angry anymore. Or not so often. Or tried not to be. But I found bird anger inexplicably funny. And anyway, anger is exhausting. I told the birds I would bring them birdseed if they told me funny things.

A tūī and a kākā landed in the same kōwhai. They hopped from flower to flower, getting nectar and yelling at each other. The kākā said, Get out! Get out!'

He sounded like a Yorkshireman, all glottal stops and no enunciation. I didn't mind the yelling. Somebody stealing your nectar *is* something to be angry about. There's someone to blame for your unhappiness after all.

It's hard to be angry when there's no one to blame. You can be angry if there's no one to blame but it's better to have a target, something to aim at, otherwise it just swishes around everywhere, like bird shit in the swimming pool, making everyone unhappy.

Ivan asked me what I'd done each day and I'd say I'd watched the birds. He knew I had a thing against birds though, so he looked for some hidden meaning.

There wasn't any.

Well, I think there wasn't. Maybe there was. Maybe, I thought, if I could learn to like something I hated, like birds, then I could learn to live with something I dreaded, like death.

Or something.

Ivan brought home a birding book he'd saved from the skip where the university library regularly dumped books. I didn't want to touch it. It was somehow like the blackbird body the cat had recently left on the bed. But Ivan looked hopeful, so I picked it up. He wouldn't talk about babies but would natter on about birds if I let him.

I didn't want to talk about birds, but we needed a language in common. I thanked him quietly and moved away towards the bush, book in hand.

I'll feed you if you stop flying away screeching, I said. I had dragged a bag of Ivan's porridge up the hill and sat throwing handfuls around.

The birds stayed away.

I thought about the birds I'd heard talk. They are not like parrots or lyrebirds or even tūī who learn to mimic human language. These were birds who uttered their own sounds and I heard them as my language. I thought about the moreporks in our suburb and the words we heard.

Birds are not supposed to swear or say anything unpleasant. They are up in the trees almost as though they've been placed on pedestals. One of The Mincing Mockingbird's birds said, I'd sell you to Satan for one corn chip. Another said, I meditate for a 15-minute break from this shitshow.

Their phrases are nothing like the birds' actual sounds, but I laugh. I don't like to put lovers or friends or family up on pedestals because they'll eventually fall off and if you're standing underneath it tends to hurt.

Birds too shouldn't be treated as pure beings. They can be arseholes too. I have a scar on my finger where the cockatoo bit it and I've seen drunk kererū fall out of trees looking like any other deadbeat on Courtenay Place on a Friday night. But the anger in their phrases made me laugh in a way that nothing else could at that time.

I opened Ivan's birding book. It covered birds from all over the world so there were birds I had neither seen nor heard, nor heard of. In it the phrases of birds were supposed to echo the sounds of the birdsongs or calls, much like the morepork saying its name in English or te reo Māori, or saying, Arsehole!

I read that in England the Common Reed Bunting says, Hello, hello, hello, piss off!

The iNdian Peacock says, Fuck off! Fuck off!

But also calls, Come back! Come back!

It's like me and Ivan. We drive each other

away then call each other back. Back and forth. Again and again.

I looked for birds from New Zealand and found an exotic one that popped across our fence from time to time from the sheep farm, the California quail. I'd heard people say that they hear the call as, Chicago! But I always thought the local ones said, Otago!

I looked it up in Ivan's book. Apparently, it says, Ah, fuck no!

It's more at home in this neighbourhood than I thought.

I'd read an article in a psychology journal on how swearing makes you feel better by releasing endorphins. So, I spent the morning imitating birds.

Later it was earthquake weather. There were no birds singing, none to listen to, no songs for me to imagine what they were saying. It was just me and the trees.

I was reading *A Field Book to Wild Birds and their Music* by Schuyler Mathews. He'd painstakingly written birdsong in musical notation and compared different birdsongs with specific snippets from opera and other scores. Every now and then he'd write the lyrics he imagined hearing too. I closed the book and thought of the black-throated green warbler in America saying,

Trees, trees, murmuring trees.

I flitted between anger and stillness. Sometimes I sat under different trees listening to them speak. The sound used to seem be a rustling of leaves but now had turned into something else. The pine trees spoke like spectres in B grade movies, and the black beech trees whispered like sorority sisters. They never used to speak to me like that. My feelings towards the forest were metamorphosing.

I took oats to the birds all week but no luck.

Ivan wanted to know why his rolled oats, which I don't eat, were disappearing. I shrugged my shoulders.

I could've told him, but I also couldn't. The vibrating of my vocal cords might have shaken me apart.

But his question stirred something in my brain, so as soon as he'd gone to work I flicked through a book and found that the native birds wanted insects, nectar, fruit, and foliage. Not grain. Not bread.

I picked up an orange from the fruit bowl and cut it in half. I filled a bottle with sugar and water. I climbed through the supplejack which was both a hindrance and a help as while I could pull on it to lever me up, I had to clamber over or under it in other places. I found a spot under a hundred-year-old beech tree. I liked the beech trees because there was less undergrowth, so it was easier to find somewhere to sit. The pines too have little undergrowth, so they easily provide dry places to hunker down, but the pines feel lifeless somehow. Perhaps because the filtered light through beech leaves is speckled and colourful like the effect of textured glass on a view, whereas pines are like shutters, shutting out the light making the forest floor look dead and deserted.

Under the tree I found a stick and pushed it into the earth and stuck half an orange onto the tip, flesh facing up. Then I sat down nearby and held the other half in my hand.

I'll feed you, I said out loud. If you stop screeching, if you come and visit.

The forest was still.

I don't know why I wanted the birds to come and feed. I don't know if I really did want the birds to come and feed. But I felt like I needed to give something back to the forest, like the laws of reciprocity had been enacted and I needed to share something in response to being given a place to sit.

I opened Ivan's book. There was a section about call and response. That's like give and receive I thought, so I turned to that chapter.

Lots of birds give warnings. The pied chat from Papua New Guinea says, *B nak ok asaw nep yj yj wkñ?* (That man of yours is coming, shall I tell him your name, or not?)

That's nice, I thought. It sounded like when my Irish colleague spotted Ivan approaching my office and said, Yer man is coming.

If I spoke Kalam I should reply, *Mnm nak apan yk manŋbyn-o, kab Kon kab ptg pwg-gp yj yj wkaŋ*, (Yeah, you're talking, but I can't hear you. Tell me his name again, and say it properly, and if the River Kon is too noisy pounding on the rocks and I don't hear you, just say the name again, would you.)

I know that feeling. When the traffic starts on its way home in the evenings the sound is like a river after rainfall, steadily increasing, growing louder, more frantic. It was that sound that told me when I'd been sitting in the bush all day and if I didn't go home soon Ivan would arrive to find me missing and he'd worry. If I left it too late the traffic was like a flooded river, angry and dangerous looking.

Never cross a swollen river.

Ivan told me his dad always feigned deafness when his mum asked anything to give him time to formulate his answer. He told me this but then tried using the same technique on me. It made me furious. The listener in PNG tries the same approach on the pied chat and I wonder if it gets furious too. Does it jump up and down angrily on a branch chirping loudly?

The pied chat then tells the listener the name of the approaching man. That would be handy, I thought. Ivan and I wouldn't have to rely on phone calls to tell us to hide behind the sleepout, or I wouldn't have to hide under my covers when someone knocked on the door even though it might be the district nurse come to check on me. I needed a pied chat perched on the deck railings to tell me who was coming up the path.

Or there is the loon who calls, Where are you?

And the mate replies with, I'm over here, where are you?

Around and around it goes. I can sympathise. Ivan and I have whole conversations like that, when we do talk, so I wonder what is the point? We don't speak the same language. He speaks Russian and I speak English, but together we now speak a pseudo English that is devoid of nuance and feeling.

How are you?

Fine thanks and you?

I'm fine thank you and you?

Around and around it goes.

I turned to the section about call and response between different species. In southern Africa the female insingizi/southern ground hornbill says in Zulu, *Ngi y' emuka, ngi y' emuka, ngi ya kwabetu,* (I'm going, I'm going home to my family)

And the male responds with, *Hamba, hamba, kad' u tsho,* (Yeah, yeah, you always say that).

Birds have the same conversations

people have. Nothing is original. If I didn't get home before Ivan did, he'd assume I'd gone to my mother's and call her.

I felt like I'd accidently entered sessions on systematic desensitisation. I loved the bush and hated the birds. Except I could now read about the birds without screwing up my face in disgust. That's a kind of call and response in itself. The birds called to me out of the pages and I responded with curiosity instead of revulsion.

A silvereye landed on the side of the orange and looked at me. Its name in te reo Māori is tauhou, newcomer. It looked at me in a way that made me feel uneasy. It's like a picture in a book, I told myself, only it's moving.

Another one landed on the opposite of the orange and they took turns pecking at it and watching me. I looked down at my hand. I saw I had been holding the other half in my hand all morning and sticky streams of juice had run down my arm and dried up. I licked my arm carefully then started to eat the orange, suddenly feeling hungry. We all fed on orange. The birds watching me as I watched the birds.

Escaping into the bush had become a habit. I couldn't remember if I had enjoyed it before. It was like I had an old video tape where the sound no longer worked and the picture was distorted. I could see the pictures moving but had no idea what anyone was saying. I could recollect heading into the bush in the past, but I had no access to the feelings I'd had. Was it joy or fear or anger? I didn't know.

In the beginning I headed up to the bush empty handed, with nothing to trade, to eat, to keep me warm. I went into the bush, I sat, I went home again, hours having passed.

Later, I'd take a bag with me containing a picnic blanket, a flask, Ivan's birding book, a bird guide, Ivan's binoculars, a fold up umbrella, a lunchbox to fill. I probably looked prepared, like an enthusiast perhaps, but I felt like a refugee fleeing. I'd grab some essentials and run into the bush without looking back.

I used to sit all day in the bush and not think of food. Then, when I started taking fruit and sugar water, I'd pour the sugar water into the basin of orange peel left from the day before and put a fresh orange on a stick next to it. When I ran out of oranges, I used a jam lid, balancing it in the crook of a branch of a kawakawa tree. When I finished setting up the feeding station, I felt hungry and started eating.

I ate and ate.

Back when the meals had appeared daily on my doorstep, I ate very little. And when they stopped appearing, I was hungry again. I ate until I felt sick then slept under the trees for a while.

I slept a lot.

One day asleep under a miro tree I was woken by a thud. When I opened my eyes there was a dazed looking kererū flapping in front of my face. It stopped moving and we looked at each other in surprise. It tried to take off but miscalculated, readjusted, tried again, and beat its wings until it reached a low hanging branch where it wobbled for a while, wings outstretched. I realised it was drunk.

I opened my book and looked up kererū. Clumsy, drunk, gluttonous, and glamorous, it said.

I laughed. I wouldn't mind being the first three if I was also glamorous. The kererū turned to look at me and almost lost its balance again. It looked up at a higher branch and extended its wings.

If I were you, I said, I'd stay where you are. For the moment at least.

I took an apple from my bag, twisted it in half and pushed one half on to the stick stuck in the ground. I ate the other half while rifling through the bag to see what else I'd brought.

There was a box of crackers, a muesli bar, a blackened banana, a bag of uncooked pasta, none of which I remembered packing. I held the pasta in my hands trying to remember why I'd put it in the backpack. I couldn't. I didn't know. If I'd had string, I could have made a necklace, or with paint and glue, a picture.

I didn't want uncooked pasta. I wanted vodka or rum or something numbing.

The kererū was sleeping. I wanted to sleep but I couldn't anymore, so I opened my book.

The nene/chanting scrub hen from Papua New Guinea says, *Ne mayabɛ,* (I'm hungry).

Me too, I said.

The acadian says it wants, Pizza!

The American goldfinch prefers a, Potato chip!

I thought of how a turkey says, Gobble, gobble, gobble.

That's how I felt. I vacuumed down the food in my bag, all except the pasta. Some silvereyes came to eat the apple. Then a big noisy tūī landed on the orange to drink the sugar water, scaring them away. A tūī eats the way I eat. In my garden it sucks the nectar from a flax flower keeping an eye out for anyone else approaching, jumping from flower to flower barely taking a breath.

I read about the northern cardinal and how it says, Dorito Dorito Dorito.

I don't usually like Doritos, but I wanted to feed chip after chip into my mouth like a kererū stuffs its mouth with kōwhai flowers. I wanted to drink like a tūī guzzles nectar and be drunk enough to fall out of a tree like a kererū and just not care.

But I was sitting in the bush with nothing left but a bag of uncooked pasta. Of all the things it is the bag of uncooked pasta that made me cry the most.

The bush is a great place to cry as spreading snot and tears everywhere is somehow perfectly fine in a way that in a house it is not. It's organic. It's part of life, or death. But the bush also doesn't care. There are no tissues or kind words or even uncomfortable silences. You are crying. So what? I could eat or drink or cry myself silly and nothing would care.

The next day I take nothing. No food, no drink. Just my eyes.

I opened my book at the section on *seeing and looking*. The brown creeper in America says, See all the big trees, see see.

I put down the book and looked. I had heard the trees but now I really looked. Black beech trunks are about a metre in diameter, which is why I had often used them to lean on when sitting on the forest floor. Beech bark is covered in black sooty velvety mould. It is both luscious and vaguely sinister looking, a cross between a filthy fireplace and an elegant armchair. This impression was bolstered when I noticed the tree appeared to be bleeding, a red sap seeping out from a damaged bit of bark. Had I hurt it? Was the tree bleeding because of me using this as a place to rest?

I felt myself retreating inward. I immediately felt hungry and tired. But I looked again and saw an insect feeding on the sap. The circle of life.

I resumed reading.

I looked up and saw a riroriro so looked it up in the book. The riroriro says, What are you doing, sit-sit-sit-sitting there?

I don't know, I replied.

It was a tiny camouflaged body in the treetops. In te reo Māori the name is the same as the call, the bird says, Riroriro riroriro, (Gone gone, gone gone).

I know he's gone, I said.

My baby is gone gone, gone gone. He too was tiny. His body weighed only 1.7 kgs and he could've lain in the crook of my arm if he hadn't been attached to monitors and drips. He too bled red droplets when they inserted needles and his blood didn't clot properly and he wouldn't stop bleeding.

Everything reminded me of him. I was

long past denial, but the acceptance of his death came and went, like the breeze, like the sounds in the leaves.

I read on. The hermit thrush says, Why don't you come to me.

He sometimes sings, Here I am right near you.

The tauhou was looking at me with his head on its side, eyes round, peering, like he understood or agreed.

In the preface of the book there was a prayer:

Whakaangi mai rā, e tama, me he manu.
Mairātia iho te waha kai rongorongo ē hei
whakaoho pō i ahau ki te whare rā.

Come to me my son, as a bird.
Come to the house and sing to me
And keep me awake at night.

I had never considered reincarnation seriously before. I didn't know if I believed in it or God or gods, but I wept when I read this, wanting it to be true. I wondered if it is the gods of this land I should be praying to or the gods of my ancestors, and if my ancestors, which ones? How far back should you go when looking for gods to pray to?

If my son was reincarnated would he be in the body of a native bird or an exotic bird? Would he be a tauhou? A stranger? A newcomer? A new friend? Not endemic, but blown here in a storm. So native, not exotic. Or are all birds born here children of this land?

I wanted more than anything for my son to perch on a branch and sing to me.

I suddenly felt a love for the bird perched, feathers fluttering softly in the breeze, tail moving to keep its balance. The science-loving part of my brain said it wasn't my son, but I wanted this bird to be him so badly that I loved the bird anyway. I loved the bird even if he was a reincarnation of someone else's child, or even if he was just a bird. The bird had a tiny heart and tiny lungs just like my son had. Somehow that was enough to recognise our common likeness, our shared mortality.

There was a bird on a branch, and it was beautiful.

The red-eyed vireo says, You see it, you hear it, you know it, you feel it, what of it?

What of it indeed, I though. As though seeing, hearing, knowing, feeling is nothing. But it is everything. I didn't notice any of it before and now I do and that is something. I don't know what, exactly.

Not yet.

It was late, and I had forgotten to go home. Ivan called out from down in the valley. He called into the bush.

I'm here, where are you?

I heard his words and thought, you silly old fool, you loon, I love you. I thought I should call out the same, I'm here, where are you?

But we would call back and forth like that, getting nowhere. I felt like we had been doing that for months, talking across each other, speaking without listening.

I stumbled down the hill, past the sooty beech and fragrant pines, the honeydew and beech sap like blood, the riroriro and tūī and tauhou and kākā, past the fungi and ferns and mosses and moulds. I swung on supplejack and stumbled to the side of the road, where the bush becomes suburbia. I saw Ivan standing on the top step looking worried.

It was time for me to call like the honey guide, singing,

Look! Look! Look! Oh! Person with wings, look! Here I come!

www.ingramcontent.com/pod-product-compliance
Lightning Source LLC
Chambersburg PA
CBHW022021290426
44109CB00015B/1261